Teddy Bear Nightmare
By: Jayde Smith

Edited by: Alexis Hance
Cover Art by: TaVaughn Speaks

DEDICATION

I would like to dedicate my first book to my mother Alexis Hance, columnist for S.W.I.F.T Magazine. She was the inspiration for me to make this book possible and was always there to support me. And to future young writers and editors across the world, may you find happiness in this journey. Thank you for choosing Teddy Bear Nightmare. I hope you enjoy reading about the mysteries of the unknown.

BIRTHDAY CHRONICLES

Happy Birthday to you!" echoed through the neighborhood as family and friends gathered to celebrate Elizabeth's sweet sixteen. Elizabeth was a sassy girl with short, curly brown hair and teal braces. Her personality was vibrant and full of energy, always the life of the party with her infectious laughter and witty remarks. Despite her braces, she had a confident smile that lit up the room whenever she entered.

The birthday party was Big Lit, held in the backyard decorated with colorful banners, fairy lights, and a large banner that read " Sweet 16 Elizabeth!" Tables were covered with teal and silver decorations, and there was a lot of delicious food and a cake with candles shaped like the number 16. Friends and family mingled, sharing stories and laughter, while upbeat music played in the background.

Elizabeth's mood was one of excitement and happiness. Her popularity showed as she was surrounded by her loved ones, enjoying their company and feeling the warmth of their affection on her special day.

Earlier that day, Elizabeth had been at school at Jefferson High School for a few hours before heading home. She generally liked school and had a good day, catching up with friends between classes and receiving warm birthday wishes from classmates and teachers alike. As she walked down the empty hallway towards her locker, located near the school exit, she couldn't shake a feeling of unease— a cold chill that made her feel as though someone was watching her, a presence like a shadow.

She turned around, half- expecting to see someone there, but the hallway remained deserted. Shrugging off the eerie sensation, she continued her way, eager to get home and start celebrating her birthday.

The walk home took her through a peaceful suburban neighborhood, with neatly trimmed lawns and blooming gardens lining the sidewalks. As she approached her house, she noticed a strange man sitting outside, as if waiting for her. He had a distinct limp and dragged his left foot, his pale skin standing out against his dark brown, somewhat unkempt hair. He was tall and wore worn- out clothes that hung loosely on his frame. There was a faint, peculiar smell about him, like old leather and damp earth.

Approaching her, he handed her a teddy bear with a raspy voice, wishing her a Happy Birthday before walking away. The teddy bear, brown and slightly worn, had a mysterious red eye that glowed faintly. Elizabeth took it hesitantly, feeling a mix of curiosity and unease at the unexpected gift and the strange encounter.

Little did she know, this birthday would turn out to be unforgettable for reasons beyond celebration— a twist of fate that would unfold later that night, changing everything she knew about that seemingly ordinary day.

She stands, hunched over the bathtub, and turns on the shower. As the water begins to flow, Elizabeth turns around to grab her favorite blue washcloth hanging on the hook. Suddenly, the shower abruptly turns off. She frowns and tries to turn the knob back and forth, but it stubbornly refuses to budge. Grabbing her matching towel, she wraps herself in it and heads downstairs to check the plumbing.
As she enters the backroom, a sudden sound catches her attention— the shower has mysteriously turned

back on. Puzzled, Elizabeth cautiously returns upstairs, standing at the bathroom door for a moment
before deciding to continue with her shower.

Later, in her bedroom, Elizabeth slips into her
blue and white pajama pants adorned with small owls
and a white tank top. She returns to the bathroom to
brush her teeth and ties her hair into a ponytail. Plac-
ing the teddy bear given to her by the strange man
on her nightstand, she climbs into bed and drifts off
to sleep.

Hours later, Elizabeth awakens to a noise downstairs.
Assuming it's her parents, she descends the stairs,
only to find the house eerily empty. Her eyes scan the
room, and she notices the teddy bear sitting in the
kitchen next to a gleaming silver kitchen knife. Feeling frightened and confused, Elizabeth picks up the
teddy bear by its arm and hurries back upstairs.

The next morning, as she prepares for school, Elizabeth hears her mother sobbing loudly on the couch,
clutching a note in her hand." What's wrong, Mom?"
Elizabeth asks, concerned. Linda hands her daughter

a sheet of loose- leaf paper with hastily scrawled handwriting:

"Dear Linda, I have taken your husband... If you wish to see him again, I'm going to need a favor in return. Decide and meet me at the house where it all began at 12:00 AM SHARP tomorrow!"

Elizabeth drops the paper in shock. Looking up at her mother, she asks, " What do they mean, ' where it all started'? "Linda looks troubled. " I don't know," she admits quietly, her mind racing. After a moment, her face lights up with realization. "Wait, I think I've figured it out!" "What is it?" Elizabeth presses eagerly. "A few years ago, the man who sold us this house... He was always a bit strange, but we needed a home," Linda begins, her voice trembling. " After we moved in, he started showing up uninvited, even making advances towards me. He seemed jealous of our family, and it escalated... He tried to... to..." Her voice trails off, choked with emotion.

Elizabeth listens in shock, piecing together the unsettling events. "He tried to kill Dad," she finishes softly, her heart pounding with fear and anger. "We had no other choice but to leave the house! When you were born, we moved to this town and started a new life." Elizabeth's world shattered when her mother uttered the unthinkable: "We must go back to that house to find your father!" Those words stung like a venomous snake bite slowly moving through Elizabeths, paralyzing her for just a moment.

Together, mother and daughter face the chilling reality that their peaceful home harbors dark secrets from its past, and their loved one's life hangs in the balance.

WHO IS HE?

Elizabeth's jaw dropped, but she knew she had to trust her mother. Without hesitation, they slipped into the shed, gathering essential tools: rope, shovel, axe, flashlight, gloves, and a gardening fork. The darkness outside seemed to swallow them whole as they tossed the tools into a black duffle bag. They drove to a neighborhood that looked frightening. Their car sped through deserted streets, passing abandoned houses half burned and crippled cars. The neighborhood reeked of despair.

Finally, they arrived at the forsaken house on the corner. Dead flowers surrounded it like mourners at a funeral. With hearts racing, they turned off the engine and exchanged fearful glances. They grabbed the black bag from the backseat of the car. The contents in the bag clinked ominously as they exited. They closed the car door silently and approached the front door of the creepy house.

Three deliberate knocks echoed through the silence. A blinding light burst forth from within the house. The creaking door revealed Elizabeth's father, bound and gagged with duct tape. Sweat-drenched black hair clung to his face; terror-filled eyes pleaded in a muffled voice for help. A faint glance to the right with his eyes was his only warning. But by the time they realized it, it was too late!

As darkness fell, a sudden noise shattered the still-ness. Elizabeth and her mother found themselves bound to chairs, their arms and legs secured tightly with ropes. Their relief at seeing Jason, unconscious but alive beside them, mingled with fear of their predicament. Strangely, their mouths were not taped shut, allowing them to exchange worried glances.

"Mom," Elizabeth whispered, her voice trembling, "I'm scared." Her mother managed a reassuring smile.
"It's going to be okay, baby. We'll get through this."

A tense silence enveloped them until the sound of approaching footsteps shattered it once more. A tall, gaunt figure loomed over them. It was the homeless man who had given Elizabeth a doll not long ago.

" Bob?!" Elizabeth's mother exclaimed in disbelief.
"You know him?" Elizabeth asked, her confusion deepening." He's... he's the one who sold us this house," her mother replied, her voice strained with recognition and fear.

Bob chuckled darkly. " Hello, Linda. It's been a while, though not for me. I've been watching you three ever since you moved away a decade ago. You've done well raising your daughter. Have you met my dear companion, Teddy?" As he spoke, Jason stirred awake, suddenly aware of their dire situation. He noticed their captor' s distraction and began to assess their chances of escape.

He hesitated for a moment, his mind racing with memories of the rigorous military training he had undergone just a year ago. They had taught him how to free himself from tangled ropes, and now, he relied on those skills. With gritted teeth, he managed to tear through the bindings, feeling the searing pain of rope burn on his wrists, but driven by the urgency to save his wife and daughter.

Quietly, he rose to his feet and crept towards a duffle bag nearby, spotting a hammer protruding from its side. With determined steps, he retrieved it and returned to where his loved ones were held captive." Hey Bob!" he called out sharply, swinging the hammer with force. The blow struck true, and Bob crumpled to the ground.

Jason wasted no time. With swift movements, he untied Elizabeth and Linda, his heart pounding with relief as they hurried into the waiting car. Fifteen tense minutes later, they pulled up in front of their home. They entered cautiously, scanning their surroundings before finally allowing themselves to relax. Their eyes met, and a smile of relief spread across their faces.

"I love you," Elizabeth murmured, her voice trembling with emotion.

Jason's gaze softened as he replied, "I love you both so much."

In that moment, the weight of their ordeal melted away, replaced by the warmth of their love and the profound gratitude of being together again, safe in their home.

THE END

OR IS IT!!

ABOUT THE AUTHOR

Jayde Autumn Smith, a 16-year-old native of Balti-more, Maryland, began her writing journey at just 14 years old with the creation of her debut novel, Teddy Bear Nightmare. This young author's talents extend beyond the page; she has also penned scripts for short films, showcasing her versatility and passion for storytelling.

When she's not writing or working on her film pro-jects, Jayde revels in the joys of laughter, fun, and adventure. She treasures spending quality time with family and friends, finding joy in the simple mo-ments of life. You might find Jayde quietly sketching away, lost in the calming world of her art. Her love for creating extends to both the written page and the canvas, where she explores her artistic visions.

Jayde is currently immersed in a performance art magnet high school program, where she shows her creative skills while also taking college courses for dual credits. Though she loves the thrill of cheering, her heart beats strongest for softball, a sport where her passion and dedication truly shine.

With a spirit bursting with creativity and a future full of promise, Jayde Autumn Smith is a young artist to watch.